CAROL M. HIGHSMITH AND TED LANDPHAIR

TEXAS
A PHOTOGRAPHIC TOUR

CRESCENT BOOKS

NEW YORK

FRONT COVER: San Antonio's picturesque River Walk redevelopment project turned an aging, decrepit downtown district into a vibrant tourist mecca. The tranquil path along the winding San Antonio River, fifteen feet below street level, has become a cosmopolitan subculture beneath cypress trees and exotic foliage. BACK COVER: The lazy Rio Grande River—so shallow in spots that it can be easily forded—takes on majestic proportions in Big Bend National Park. Sheer cliffs mark the Mexican side to the south. PAGE 1: The flags of the United States, Texas, and the City of Dallas, left to right, fly outside Dallas's City Hall. PAGES 2–3: Big Bend National Park is an awesome but somewhat inaccessible place, far from urban centers. There, the Chisos Mountains jut spectacularly out of the harsh Chihauhuan desert.

Photographs copyright © 1998
by Carol M. Highsmith
Text copyright © 1998
by Random House Value Publishing, Inc.

This 1998 edition is published by Crescent Books®, a division of Random House Value Publishing, Inc., 201 East 50th Street, New York, N.Y. 10022.

Crescent Books® and colophon are registered trademarks of Random House Value Publishing, Inc.

Random House
New York • Toronto • London • Sydney • Auckland
http://www.randomhouse.com/

Printed and bound in China

Library of Congress Cataloging-in-Publication Data
Highsmith, Carol M., 1946–
Texas / Carol M. Highsmith and Ted Landphair.
p. cm. — (A photographic tour)
Includes index.
ISBN 0-517-20180-1 (hc: alk. paper)
1. Texas—Tours. 2. Texas—Pictorial works.
I. Landphair, Ted, 1942– . II. Title. III. Series:
Highsmith, Carol M., 1946– Photographic tour.
F384.3.H55 1998 97–39926
917.64´0022´2—dc21 CIP

8 7 6 5 4 3 2 1

Project Editor: Donna Lee Lurker
Designed by Robert L. Wiser, Archetype Press, Inc.,
Washington, D.C.

All photographs by Carol M. Highsmith unless otherwise credited: map by XNR Productions, page 5; painting by Gwendolyn H. Branstetter Western, Wildlife, and Landscape Art, Refugio, Texas, page 6; Fort Worth Convention & Visitors Bureau, page 8; John Lovett Western History Collection, Norman, Oklahoma, page 9; Webb County Heritage Foundation, Laredo, page 10; Webb County Heritage Foundation/S. N. Johnson Collection, Laredo, page 11; Dr Pepper Museum, Waco, page 12; East Texas Research Center, Steen Library, Stephen F. Austin State University, Nacogdoches, page 13; Spindletop/Gladys City Boomtown Museum, Beaumont, page 14; East Texas Oil Museum, Kilgore, page 15; Bryce's Cafeteria, Texarkana, page 16; Houston Livestock Rodeo and Show,, page 17; The Buddy Holly Memorial Society, Wethersfield, Connecticut, page 18; The Roy Orbison Museum, Wink, Texas, page 19; Arlington Convention & Visitors Bureau, page 20; Vernon J. Biever Collection, Port Washington, Wisconsin, page 21

THE AUTHORS GRATEFULLY ACKNOWLEDGE
THE SUPPORT PROVIDED BY

HILTON HOTELS CORPORATION

AND

THE ARLINGTON HILTON
THE AUSTIN NORTH HILTON AND TOWERS
THE EL PASO AIRPORT HILTON
THE HILTON PALACIO DEL RIO, SAN ANTONIO
THE UNIVERSITY HILTON, HOUSTON

IN CONNECTION WITH THE COMPLETION
OF THIS BOOK

THE AUTHORS ALSO WISH TO THANK
THE FOLLOWING FOR THEIR GENEROUS
ASSISTANCE AND HOSPITALITY
DURING THEIR VISITS TO TEXAS

Chinos Mountain Lodge, Big Bend National Park; Fairfield Inn, Abilene; Hardeman House, Nacogdoches; Holiday Inn Civic Center, Lubbock; The Mansion on Main, Texarkana; The Radisson Inn, Amarillo; Travelers Inn, Brownsville

Abilene Convention & Visitors Bureau; Amarillo Convention and Visitor Council; Arlington Convention & Visitors Bureau; Austin Convention & Visitors Bureau; Beaumont Convention & Visitors Bureau; Brownsville Convention & Visitors Bureau; Corpus Christi Convention & Visitors Department; Dallas Convention & Visitors Bureau; Del Rio Chamber of Commerce; Denton Convention & Visitor Bureau; El Paso Convention and Visitors Bureau; Fort Stockton Department of Tourism; Fort Worth Convention & Visitors Bureau; Fredericksburg Convention & Visitors Bureau; Galveston Convention & Visitors Bureau; Greater Houston Convention and Visitors Bureau; Irving Convention & Visitors Bureau; Laredo Convention and Visitors Bureau; Convention and Tourism Bureau of Lubbock; McAllen Convention & Visitors Bureau; Midland Chamber Convention and Visitors Bureau; Odessa Convention and Visitors Bureau; Nacogdoches Convention & Visitors Bureau; San Angelo Convention & Visitors Bureau; San Antonio Convention & Visitors Bureau; Texarkana Chamber of Commerce; Texas Department of Economic Development, Tourism Division

Sally Alvis, Nacogdoches; Kimberley R. Baker, Austin; Gabe Bustamante, United States Border Patrol, McAllen Sector; Chris Castillo, Beaumont; Stuart Daniels, Texarkana; Elise Eustace, Lubbock; Mona Gandy, Irving; Christine Schmidt Heimann, Fredericksburg; Cathy Henry, The King Ranch; Dr. Jere Jackson, Stephen F. Austin State University, Nacogdoches; Jeff Johnston, Brownsville; Susan Cottle Leonard, Del Rio; Shura Lindgren, Midland; Eric W. Miller, Amarillo; Pat Owsley, Odessa; Judy Everett Ramos, Arlington; Vince Scolaro, Dallas; Brad Smyth, Austin; C. Greg Staley, Fort Worth; Francisco Tamez, Laredo; Carla Torres, Houston; Debbie Vickers, Odessa; Shawn Withington, McAllen; Donna Yecke, El Paso

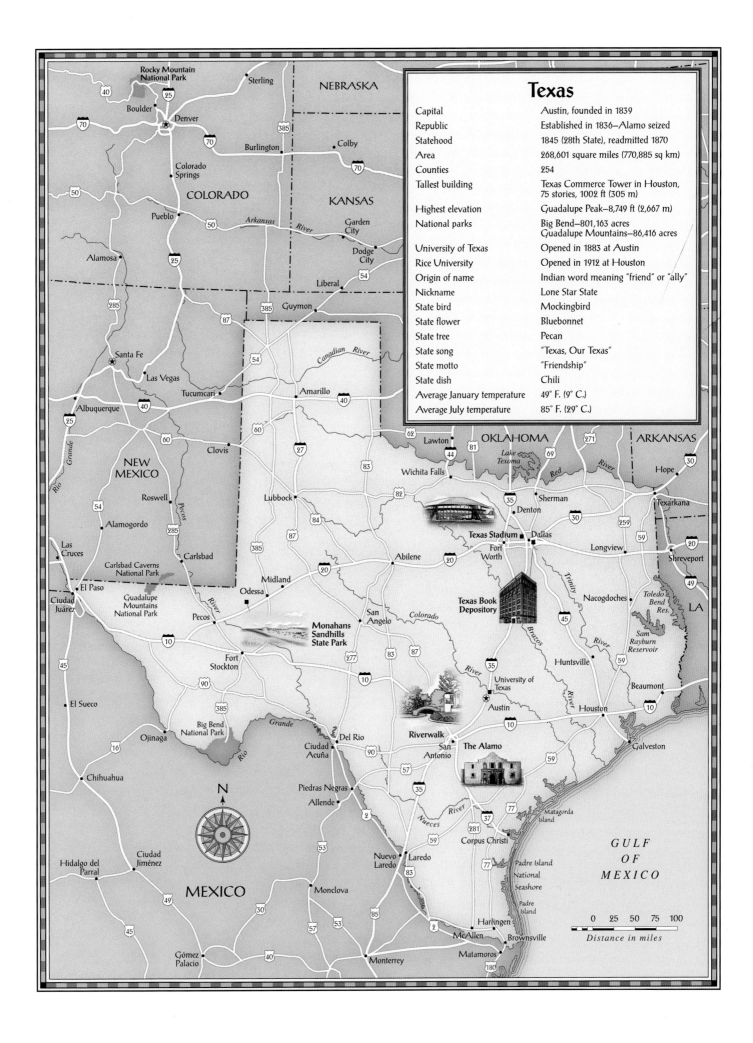

TEXAS. THE VERY NAME SUMMONS A FLOOD OF IMAGES: A lone star. Rolling skies. Tumbling tumbleweeds. The Panhandle, the Chisholm Trail, and the Rio Grande. Lumbering longhorns, lonesome cowhands, and Texas Rangers. String ties, Stetson hats, and six-guns. Five-card draw and two-steps. Gushers, stockyards, stockbrokers, big money, and big deals. Hot chili, barbecue joints, and hot salsa. Lyndon and Lady Bird. Holly, Orbison, and good-ol' Bob Wills. *The Last Picture Show.* The 'Boys. "Remember the Alamo!" And so on, for Texas is a *big* state with an almost endless catalogue of sights, sounds, and memorable people and places.

Imagine New York, New Jersey, Pennsylvania, Ohio, Illinois, *and* the six New England states. Texas is bigger than all of them put together. In the late 1930s, a writer trying to capture the enormity of Texas asked readers to imagine a hinge at the top of the Panhandle, one at the eastern border with Louisiana, and another at the western tip. He pointed out that if you lift the northern hinge, Brownsville, the southernmost point of the continental United States, would land within 120 miles of Canada. Fold Texas to the east and El Paso would be forty miles short of the Atlantic Ocean. Flip the state westward and Orange, Texas, would fall 215 miles out into the Pacific.

When Texas was willingly annexed into the United States in 1845—the only sovereign republic ever to enter the Union—the treaty stipulated that, at any time it wanted to, Texas could break into as many as five separate states. It has at least that many distinctive topographies—piney woods, brushy hill country, scrubby rangeland, languid seashore, and verdant bayous among them—and, in addition, an admixture of different and diverse cultures. It is a testament to the remarkable solidarity of Texans that no such effort to subdivide the state has ever been proposed seriously.

Drive through parts of Austin and you may swear you could be in the Silicon Valley. Dallas may feel like Denver, or Houston like Atlanta, or Galveston like New Orleans. The state's bayous may suggest Louisiana Cajun country and its desert could well be in Nevada. The antebellum mansions in Columbus or Corpus Christi may well remind one of Natchez or Vicksburg, and there's no telling North Texas or southern Oklahoma apart. And Texarkana even spills into another state—Arkansas. But in all these places, despite superficial resemblances, there's never a doubt you're in Texas.

That's because a citizen from Texas in chaps or fine-wool slacks, jeans or designer clothes, seems to radiate a *Texan* identity. It is an aura that traces to *Tejas*—an Indian word meaning "friend" or "friendship." A Texan in New York or Rangoon might be detected by the trace of distinctive twang in his or her speech, but is much more readily spotted by an outgoing nature. Walk down a Texas street and people will say hello. Drive down a Texas lane and folks will wave. Lean over a cup of coffee at a diner and someone will strike up a conversation. A stranger is "sir" or "ma'am," and an offer of help or a friendly word is sure to be genuine.

Texans don't merely preach these old-fashioned, good-hearted values, they live them. Self-reliance is in their blood, but standoffishness is not. A Texan from Amarillo is 750 miles from a Texan in McAllen. One from Orange is 850 miles from a Texan in El Paso. And they work in a variety of occupations from raising cattle, grapefruit, cotton, and pecan trees, to picking beans, branding steers, and dealing oil futures. So Texans know the meaning of "diversity" and knew the meaning of the word long before it became fashionable. They also understand the necessity of compromise: Do what it takes to get a job done. On the open range, far from town, neighbors

Barren and brown, save for its piney woods and bayous, much of Texas erupts into a panoply of colors come springtime. Notably, a carpet of bluebonnets—the state flower—bursts to life. The silky flowering herb is a favorite subject of Gwendolyn Branstetter, the acclaimed landscape artist from Refugio, Texas.

Butch Cassidy (lower right) and the Sundance Kid— Harry Longabaugh (lower left)— pose brazenly with their "Wild Bunch" gang of bank robbers in Fort Worth. A Pinkerton agent saw the photo and chased them from town.

needed each other's help stringing fences, mounting posses, or raising barns. Water, well before oil, was precious, and when a stranger stopped at your well after a long, hard ride, you welcomed him and offered a meal. Glad to help. No questions asked and nothing expected in return.

Tejas. Friendship.

Texans have been open to different people and new ideas because they have always lived on the edge of the Spanish world, the French world, the Anglo world, and on the very brink of the untamed American frontier. Texans are proud of their history, but not mired in it. Living where "seldom is heard a discouraging word," they have always thought positively, welcomed change, and taken risks.

It's true that Texans have been known to "brag on" their state, or their town, but not so often about themselves—despite the exaggerated stereotypes of the TV series *Dallas*. It's no coincidence that just about every Texas town has a business with the word "Big" in it: The Big State. The Big Texan. Big John's. Big's not swagger in Texas, son, it's fact and you'd best think big, too. Even country roads are big. They're called "farm to market roads," marked "FM," and they're as long, straight, wide, and well maintained as U.S. highways. The foresight of building such fine, fast roads helped put Texas farm goods on tables across America. But as the history of the Lone Star State will show, foresight was only part of it. With its tough, larger-than-life heroes, Texas, from the beginning, was destined to go places.

In 1519—six years after Juan Ponce de León discovered Florida and more than a century before English colonists established Jamestown in Virginia—Spanish explorer Alonso Alvarez de Pineda first mapped the Texas coastline and sailed partway up the Rio Grande. But for two centuries, fierce resistance from natives—whom the Spanish were trying to enslave as they

searched for gold and treasure—kept Spain from establishing much of a foothold in the terri-tory above the Rio Grande. The expeditions by the *conquistador* Francisco Cortez de Coronado, explorer Hernando de Soto, and others continued, but it was only after the great French pathfinder Robert Cavelier de La Salle founded a fort and small colony in Matagorda Bay in 1685 that Spain, in order to blunt the French incursion, began settlement in earnest.

The Spanish built a string of missions and *presidios*—or forts—to protect them. Nacog-doches—one of the first true towns in what would be Texas—located on the nebulous western edge of a no-man's land between the Spanish and French empires, soon became the center of a lucrative, and often illegal, trade in wild horses, cattle, and smuggled goods. The clandestine road around Nacogdoches became more heavily traveled than the official trade route through the checkpoint at the Old Stone Fort where taxes were levied. An equal distance to the other side of the Sabine River, in French Louisiana, was Natchitoches. (Nacogdoches and Natchi-toches were said to be sons of the Indian chief Red Feather, who, according to legend, sent them a day's journey in each direction from the Sabine with orders to begin settlements.) It was through Nacogdoches that Spanish cattlemen surreptitiously traded with the French. It was here, too, after Mexico gained independence from Spain in 1821, that three separate efforts to establish an independent Texas were attempted *before* the Texas revolution. While six flags would ultimately fly over the rest of Texas—Spanish, French, Mexican, Texas Republic, Con-federate, and U.S.—*nine* flags, including those of the three abortive republics, would fly over Nacogdoches. In 1836, when William Travis, Jim Bowie, Davy Crockett, and more than 190 other fighting men marched to the Alamo in San Antonio to confront Antonio Lopez Santa Anna and his Mexican legions, it was Nacogdoches that financed and armed the expedition.

Crusty "Judge" Roy Bean, posturing in the saddle in front of his saloon/courtroom in Langtry, Texas, called himself "The Law West of the Pecos" and erected a sign to underscore the boast.

American adventurers had long been operating in Texas. In 1803, when the United States acquired the vast Territory of Louisiana—stretching all the way from New Orleans to the Canadian border—many American expansionists contended the border stretched west of the Sabine into Texas. Spanish troops routed some small American incursions but could not staunch the steady stream of American troublemakers called "filibusters." "G.T.T." was the saying of the day among scoundrels fleeing U.S. justice: "gone to Texas." The Spanish governor's task was complicated when the king in Madrid granted settlements to Anglo-American *empresarios*—colonizers—like Moses Austin, a Saint Louis banker, and his son Stephen. They built a whole town of fifty-six hundred Anglos on the Brazos River. After it successfully gained independence from Spain and took possession of Texas, the new Mexican Republic fared no better in controlling the American immigration problem.

Mexico considered its administration enlightened in comparison with Spanish autocratic rule, but Americans in Texas chafed at the requirement of membership in the Roman Catholic Church and the denial of rights such as trial by jury. In 1830, after the three failed attempts at revolution in Nacogdoches, Mexico banned all emigration from the United States. Before long, however, Mexican soldiers and Texas farmers were skirmishing, and not just American immigrants but also many Texas Mexicans were plotting wholesale revolution.

By this time, Sam Houston, a former U.S. congressman and governor of Tennessee, was living in Nacogdoches. After divorcing his wife and, for a time, living among the Cherokee Indians, he headed west in search of adventure and land. In the meantime, Stephen Austin was nagging the Mexican authorities about civil rights and firebrands like Travis and Bowie were openly agitating for independence. In 1835, Santa Anna became Mexican *presidente* and immediately

Laredo's city hall, built in 1883–84, housed government offices, a performing-arts center, and El Mercado— an open-air market. A tower and cupola were later added to "Market Hall."

assumed dictatorial powers. Weary of the complaining of the Texans, he sent troops northward to oust the agitators. But before they could arrive en masse, Texans under Bowie and James Fannin Jr. roused the Mexican garrisons of Gonzales, Goliad, and finally San Antonio. Houston spread posters throughout the United States that promised land to volunteers who would come to help fight the "usurper." Santa Anna flew into a rage and threatened to "march through [the Americans'] own country and plant the Mexican flag in Washington." He personally took command of the Mexican force and advanced to reclaim San Antonio.

What resulted, as every Texas schoolchild knows, was the Battle of the Alamo. Five thousand Mexican troops, after prolonged bombardment and fearful hand-to-hand combat, wiped out Travis, Crockett, and the rest of the tiny force of "Texians" (the term would not be commonly simplified as "Texans" until Texas joined the Union in 1845) who had turned the mission into a makeshift fort. Four days earlier, a declaration of Texan independence had been adopted in the town of Washington on the Brazos River—a constitution followed less than two weeks after the Alamo slaughter. Santa Anna confidently moved his troops eastward to complete the annihilation but ran into Sam Houston and a fair-sized army on the San Jacinto River. The Texians shouted "Remember the Alamo!" as they attacked the Mexican legions during their siesta and completely routed them. Santa Anna was captured and thousands of Mexicans were either killed or captured. Texas had won its independence.

Houston was chosen president of the new republic, with instructions to immediately begin discussions about eventual annexation into the United States. It was clear from the start that Texas could not endure as a separate nation. It lacked good farmland and many natural resources (oil had not yet been discovered), and it was financially threadbare from its fight for

San Agustin Church in Laredo had only recently been completed in the early 1880s when the volunteer fire department gathered on the plaza for a fire drill to test the city's new hydrants.

Dr Pepper was concocted in Waco's Old Corner Drug Store, where the soft drink was first called a "Waco." It was a hit, and was soon bottled in a big plant in town.

independence. And, of course, it faced the real threat of reprisals from Mexico. Nevertheless, its sovereignty was soon recognized by the United States and several European nations. The Texas Republic established a government and the Texas Rangers, a western-style armed force to protect the frontier from Mexicans, outlaws, and raiding Indians.

The republic lasted almost a decade. Its citizens were anxious to join the United States, but the feeling was not entirely mutual. Slavery had become a contentious issue and resulted in the defeat of the first treaty of annexation proposed in the Senate because of the fear of adding another slave state to the Union. But wagon trains were already rolling into Texas and railroads were making plans to follow. Soon the ties between the expansionist United States and its new southwest neighbor were growing too strong to resist. Soon after Democrat James K. Polk took back the White House from the Whigs in the 1844 presidential election, largely on a platform of bringing Texas into the Union, both houses of Congress adopted a resolution to admit Texas as the twenty-eighth state.

If Mexico had difficulty in dealing with Texas as a rebel republic, it regarded its annexation by the United States as a hostile declaration of war. While the Texas Republic had not bothered to colonize much below the Nueces River leading to Corpus Christi, Polk and his expansionist supporters admitted a new state of Texas that extended all the way south to the Rio Grande River, territory they intended to seize. Mexican troops attacked, but a well-armed force led by General Zachary Taylor soon marched, with very little difficulty, across the border and drew a bead on Mexico City. The Mexicans quickly capitulated.

On February 2, 1848, with the Treaty of Guadalupe Hidalgo, the United States acquired not only Texas—whose "panhandle" at the time reached far north into present-day Colorado and

Kansas—but also vast territory south of the forty-second parallel all the way to the Pacific Ocean (later New Mexico, Arizona, and the southernmost portion of California). Thinking big even then, the new Texas Legislature brazenly claimed parts of the present states of New Mexico, Oklahoma, Kansas, and Colorado as its own. Congress would have none of it from this new slave state, however, and set the boundaries that exist to this day in order to reserve other southwestern territory for future nonslave states.

Sam Houston, who first went to Washington as the new United States senator from Texas, returned again to run, successfully, for governor in 1858. Three years later when the state ratified an ordinance of secession in order to join the new Confederate States of America, Houston refused to sign it. He was deposed and the office was declared vacant. Houston later died in poverty in 1863. Because of its remoteness, the state was spared many engagements in the bitter Civil War. It was the Confederacy's chief conduit of cattle, cotton, and goods shipped from abroad through Mexico even after its ports were blockaded by the Union navy. The war's last land battle was fought on Palmito Hill in the Rio Grande Valley and won by Confederate forces. Unbeknownst to the combatants, Confederate commander-in-chief Robert E. Lee had surrendered at Appomattox a full month earlier.

The postwar period in Texas was devoted to dealing with the harsh terms of Reconstruction dictated by the victorious Union Army and Radical Republicans in Congress, and to taming the rangeland west of the Pecos River. The Pecos, which pokes generally northward from the Rio Grande near Del Rio, was more than a sentimental boundary between civilization and the frontier. The area possesses deep canyons that took railroads years to cross; and rainfall totals drop, almost mysteriously, from the Pecos westward. And hostile Comanches, rogue Mexicans, and American outlaws gave Texas Rangers all they could handle. Frontier justice was so desperately needed that "Judge" Roy Bean, a rotund former liquor salesman, set up a courthouse in a saloon in tiny Langtry and proclaimed himself "the law west of the Pecos." Despite the claims of the legend and the Paul Newman movie, Bean never hanged anyone. He was a simple justice of the peace who fined offenders, often spending the proceeds on drinks for the "house." Texas Rangers hauled serious offenders up to the town of Pecos for trial before a real judge.

In untamed Nacogdoches's square near the Old Stone Fort—headquarters for three early unsuccessful attempts to establish a Republic of Texas—stood a few scraggly trees in 1898. One was the town hanging tree.

With the twentieth century came advances in technology that helped Texas to modernize. The expansion of railroads, the arrival of the windmill (to pull water from deep beneath the parched desert plains), and the invention and widespread use of barbed wire (which enabled farmers to get a foothold in free-range cattle country) were all important to the burgeoning economic growth of Texas. But the most momentous development was the "discovery" of oil, which altered the course of Texas forever. Oil had lain in pools under the very noses of Texans for decades. Indians used it for potions, and it annoyed settlers who, in search of water, happened to drill through it. The first gusher was "Spindletop" near Beaumont. Soon afterward in Kilgore, what became called the "World's Richest Acre" turned Texas into a boom state. "Black gold" brought fortune, international fame, and even more larger-than-life characters. Megalopolises around Dallas and Houston soon arose as Texas became the shooting star of the exploding Sunbelt.

With money, mushrooming population, and rapidly increasing

electoral votes—in presidential elections of the 1990s, only California and New York had more—came unprecedented national political power. Republican Dwight D. Eisenhower, born in Denison, Texas, won two landslide presidential elections in the 1950s. But Ike spent most of his life in Kansas, Pennsylvania, Washington, and, of course, the battlefields of Europe, than he did in the Lone Star State. In the 1950s and early '60s in Washington, two Texans ran the Democrat-controlled Congress: "Mr. Sam" Rayburn of Bonham ruled as the Speaker of the House and Lyndon Johnson of Johnson City directed the Senate as majority leader. Johnson later became President John F. Kennedy's vice president and then president in 1963 after Kennedy's tragic assassination. In 1989, George Bush, a transplant Texan, became another vice president to rise to the presidency. In 1992, H. Ross Perot, the billionaire Texas businessman, ran the most successful (in percentage of popular votes) third-party campaign in American history.

Texans seem to speak in codes among themselves, using terms like "East Texas" and "West Texas" as if there were a definite demarcation. But is East Texas the piney woods in the corner near Arkansas, or the bayous abutting Louisiana, or sprawling Houston? Dallas and Fort Worth are east of center, but well north of South Texas, wherever that is! Where does West Texas begin? Abilene, perhaps, but that's almost 480 miles—the width of Colorado—from El Paso. Texans seem to know the answers to these questions. Like the proverbial elephant inspected by a blindfolded person, Texas is best comprehended in small sections.

The piney woods of northeast Texas share a timber economy and many cultural ties with northwestern Louisiana and southwestern Arkansas. Indeed, Louisianians have long groused that Shreveport should move into Texas and be done with it, such is that city's passion for the Dallas Cowboys football team. Texarkansans are used to geographical confusion: half of their city is in Texas and half is in Arkansas. Its three most important public buildings, including the post office, were built straddling the state line. Bowie County, Texas, is "dry" while Miller County, Arkansas, has plenty of liquor stores. Arkansas has a state income tax while Texas does not—a problem solved by a special exemption for Arkansas residents of Texarkana. H. Ross Perot is a *Texas* Texarkansan. To confuse visitors and would-be lawbreakers, the two sides of this city have separate administrations and police forces, but a bi-state justice center with unique legal jurisdictions applicable only inside the building. Because of the ever-southward shifting of the American populace, in the 1990s Texarkana has become the population center of all of North America, in addition to being a prime location for manufacturing and distribution.

Marshall, Longview, and Tyler are strung close together along Interstate 20, between Shreveport and Dallas. Marshall is the gateway to Caddo Lake State Park, a primeval place full of cypress trees trimmed with Spanish moss. From Thanksgiving to New Year's Day, the city also hosts one of the largest holiday light shows in the nation. Marshall is also the home to Marshall Pottery & Museum, established in 1896, one of the largest manufacturers of glazed pottery in the country. Longview offers comprehensive exhibits on East Texas history at the Gregg County Historical Museum and is the host of the annual Great Texas Balloon race. Tyler, since the Civil War, has called itself the "Rose Capital of the Nation." It operates the nation's largest municipal rose garden and museum. The garden blooms with thirty thousand bushes exhibiting four

When the Lucas Gusher blew on Spindletop Hill in Beaumont in 1901, a boomtown sprang up overnight, ushering in America's Energy Age. The gusher spewed for several days before the photographer caught this photo.

Text on photo: YOU WILL MEET ALL OF THE OLD BOOMERS IN KILGORE TEX / 102 / BY SKIP NOLAN

hundred varieties of roses from early May until frost. Close to all three of these cities is tiny Jefferson, a vestige of the Old South that is a favorite weekend retreat for residents of Dallas–Fort Worth. The ratio of antebellum and Greek Revival homes that have been turned into bed-and-breakfast inns—more than sixty in a town of two thousand—is one of the highest in America.

Not far to the south in East Texas are Nacogdoches and Lufkin. Nacogdoches, the oldest town in Texas by many reckonings, is considered the "cradle of Texas liberty" and has many historic attractions. Lufkin is true timber country with two national forests and the Texas Forestry Museum to prove it. Huntsville is even deeper in "Deep East Texas." It was founded in the 1830s by a man who had moved his family from Huntsville, Alabama. Sam Houston's family lived in Huntsville, Texas, too, in a plantation home south of town. A dazzling white, concrete and steel, sixty-seven-foot-high statue of the Texas statesman stands today at the Huntsville Visitor Center on Texas Highway 75. There's a Sam Houston museum and memorial park downtown, as well as the Texas Prison Museum, where captivating exhibits like Bonnie and Clyde's rifles, and "Old Sparky"—the state's actual electric chair—can be found.

Museums are the attraction in several other East Texas cities on the road to Dallas–Fort Worth as well. In Temple is the Railroad and Pioneer Museum, the centerpiece of the city's annual Texas Train Festival. In Kilgore, down the street from the park that's crammed with oil derricks to commemorate the "World's Richest Acre," are the East Texas Oil Museum, filled with memorabilia of boomtown days, and the headquarters and museum of the Kilgore Rangerettes. The Rangerettes are perhaps the nation's best-known drill team, regularly performing at Dallas Cowboy and Cotton Bowl football games. In College Station, on the campus of Texas A&M University, is the George Bush Presidential Library and Museum. Dedicated in 1997, it displays

The easygoing rural life of East Texas changed drastically with the discovery of oil during 1930 and 1931. Sleepy Kilgore became a raucous boomtown crammed with prospectors, speculators, and suppliers.

replicas of President Bush's Camp David and Air Force One offices. And in Waco are two popular museums. One is devoted to the exploits of the Texas Rangers. The other is the Dr Pepper Museum located in an old Dr Pepper bottling plant. It tells the fascinating story of the invention, production, and advertising of hundreds of American soft drinks. It was in Waco, at the Old Country Drug Store, that pharmacist Charles Curtis Alderton developed the still-secret concoction for Dr Pepper.

Swaggering Dallas is one of Texas's youngest cities. It was once a humble trading post dwarfed by Fort Worth. But the arrival of the railroads in the 1870s, the downtown Neiman-Marcus department store in 1907, a Federal Reserve bank in 1914, and Dallas Love Field airport in 1927 spurred substantial growth. However, it was the spectacular development of the East Texas Oil Field a hundred miles to the east in the 1930s that capped its dramatic expansion. Even though Dallas County itself has never had a single oil well, Dallas became the financial and technical center for the oil patch, and, in the process, one of the nation's top-five business and convention cities.

After years of shame and introspection, the nation's eighth-largest city turned the dark days that followed the assassination of President John F. Kennedy in Dealey Plaza in 1963 into an inspirational legacy. Dallas County converted the old Texas School Book Depository—from which the Warren Commission controversially concluded that Lee Harvey Oswald fired all the shots that killed Kennedy—into its administration building. Upstairs, the county's historical foundation operates a Sixth Floor Museum that recalls the life and tragic death of the president in moving photographs, film clips, exhibits, and the same view of Dealey Plaza that Oswald is said to have had.

By the late 1990s, Dallas boasted more than forty-three thousand hotel rooms, ranking second in convention and meeting attendees, and offered more restaurants per person than New

Bryce's Cafeteria in Texarkana is a Texas institution, legendary for its array of home-cooked food, including more than twenty-five varieties of pie. Bryce K. Lawrence opened for business in 1931.

York City. DFW, the airport it shares with other cities in the Metroplex (as the greater metropolitan area is known), is larger than Manhattan Island and has become the world's second-busiest, behind only Atlanta's Hartsfield Airport. Yet Dallas somehow managed to remain the least densely populated major metropolitan area in the world.

Fort Worth, the Metroplex's other anchor, cheerfully clings to its "Cowtown" nickname and image. Even its coliseum carries that name. The steers and slaughterhouses are gone from its fabled stockyards, but the National Historic District has been redeveloped into one of the state's premier entertainment and dining districts. The world's largest honky tonk (venues for "boot-scootin'" being a relatively recent world-wide category to be measured) is Billy Bob's in Fort Worth. And the Chisholm Trail, which once terminated at the Fort Worth Stockyards, is remembered with a giant mural downtown. The location is "Sundance Square," named for the Sundance Kid, who, with his pal Butch Cassidy and other assorted rapscallions, once lived and robbed banks almost openly in Fort Worth. Good-natured competition with glitzy Dallas is a Fort Worth cottage industry. "Fort Worth is where the West begins," its citizens love to quote Will Rogers. "Dallas is where the East peters out!" Sophistication is not lost on Cowtown, however; only New York and Washington's cultural districts are larger. Located in town is the Museum of Modern Art of Fort Worth, the state's oldest museum founded in 1892, as well as many other museums, galleries, and concert halls.

No longer are smaller cities surrounding Dallas–Fort Worth inconsequential dots on the map of Texas. Arlington, the "Midway of the Metroplex," is home not only to the popular Six Flags Over Texas and Six Flags Hurricane Harbor amusement parks, but also the baseball-only Ballpark in Arlington. It opened in 1994 to favorable comparisons with Baltimore and Cleveland's new parks as one of the major-leagues' most intimate and inviting new stadiums. Arlington is so trendy that, according to a local census completed in the 1990s, the median age in the fast-growing community is 29! Irving—already known as the home of the Dallas Cowboys who play at Texas Stadium—burst into its own in business circles with the development of Las Colinas, a less-congested (and less-expensive) "alternate downtown" corporate headquarters to Dallas. In Waxahachie, south of the Metroplex, and Denton, to the north, the tourism emphasis is historical. Both cities take pride in magnificent Romanesque courthouses—two of the biggest and most ornate in the nation. In Denton, visitors can see an operating, 1885-vintage hardware store and a collection of Texas First Ladies' gowns—preserved by the Daughters of the American Revolution—at Texas Woman's College. Wichita Falls, northwest of Fort Worth on the Oklahoma line, has recreated the waterfall on the Red River that gave the city its name. In 1995, the old Wichita Theater and Opera House reopened as the site of Branson-style country music shows.

Heading west, Abilene, too, has a richly restored theater, the Paramount, as well as an award-winning zoo and nature center, and an exposition center that hosts two of Texas's most historic rodeos each year. Go much farther west and south, and there's no mistaking the beginnings of West Texas: pumpjacks and chemical plants by the hundreds in the countryside. In Midland, the Museum of the Southwest features southwestern art and archaeology. In San Angelo is Fort Concho, the state's best-preserved military fort, and Miss Hattie's, a restored "ladies of the evening" saloon and "parlor house," as well as the state's best deer hunting in the surrounding

The spectacular Houston Livestock Show and Rodeo, now held at the Astrodome, puts special emphasis on the "show." Roy Rogers and Dale Evans were honorees at the rodeo in the 1950s.

Buddy Holly (center) of Lubbock became a "rockabilly" superstar before his untimely death in an airplane crash. A Buddy Holly statue and "Walk of Fame" saluting West Texas entertainers is now a Lubbock attraction.

area. Nearby in Big Spring are a pioneer heritage museum and the Comanche State Trail. In Odessa there are: a petroleum museum that traces the rich history of the Permian Basin; the Globe of the Great Southwest, a performing arts theater that's a recreation of Shakespeare's Globe; and the Presidential Museum, the only museum in the country dedicated solely to the nation's highest office. At Monahans Sandhills State Park is the beginning of a two-hundred-mile-long dune field that extends all the way into New Mexico. In Lubbock there is a ranching heritage center, a windmill museum, and a "walk of fame" that salutes "rockabilly" legend Buddy Holly and other West Texas entertainers.

The Texas Panhandle, a region the size of Indiana, is unabashed cowboy country. Cowboy hats, trophy belts, and cowboy boots are as thick as West Texas grasshoppers in Amarillo, a favorite last stop of Texans on their way to vacation in cooler and more mountainous Colorado. Even the logo of this city that calls itself the "real Texas" features cowboy boots in place of the double-L's in its name. Little wonder. In 1893, Amarillo's population was listed as "between 500–600 humans and 50,000 head of cattle"; a fourth of the nation's—and 88 percent of Texas's—beef comes from Amarillo. So flat and vast are the Great Plains beyond Amarillo that the city's airport has the world's third-longest runway. It's so endless that the runway is designated as an alternate landing site for the U.S. space shuttle.

There's another city in the "Pass of the North"—through which Spanish *conquistadores* traveled into Texas—that's so far west it's in another time zone: El Paso. Here on the Mexican border is Ysleta, the oldest mission in Texas, built in 1681. Not only are Spanish and Mexican traditions preserved in El Paso, but one of the federally recognized Native American tribes, the Tiguas, also make their home in the community of Ysleta, within the city limits. So confident are El Pasoans of their mastery of Mexican cuisine that they lay claim to the "best Mexican food in the world"—their nearby neighbor to the south notwithstanding. Spanish, Mexican, Native American, and Western American cultures are all showcased in a summertime musical pageant, *Viva El Paso!,* in an amphitheater tucked in McKelligon Canyon.

Along the Rio Grande to the south and east lies one of the nation's most spectacular national parks. It is relatively little-visited, owing to its inaccessibility and distance from major metropolitan areas and freeways. Indeed, some of its devotees say its distance from anywhere else is its greatest asset. Inhospitable Big Bend—named for the abrupt turn northward of the river beneath towering cliffs—is home to the craggy Chisos Range that rises dramatically from the Chihuahuan desert floor, as well as to exotic animals like the "red racer" coachwhip snake, the boar-like javelina, the Texas banded gecko lizard, and the Mexican gray wolf. Cactus flowers—the hot pink pitaya, golden rainbow, and red claret-cup cactus among them—which bloom later than most Texas spring flowers, set the Big Bend aglow with color. Within shouting distance of Big Bend—Texans can shout a long way—are: Del Rio, which calls itself "the best of the border"; Uvalde, where an 1891 grand opera house thrives producing community theater; Langtry, where Judge Roy Bean pined for a distant woman (English actress Lily Langtry) he would never meet; and Seminole Canyon State Historical Park, where remarkably preserved painted cave pictographs by prehistoric people have been discovered.

Texas's southernmost tail, or the "Texas Tropics," as one of its cities—McAllen—likes to call it, is a rich agricultural region, where beans, spinach, oranges, and grapefruit thrive. The destiny of border towns like Laredo and Brownsville is intertwined with their Mexican neighbors across the Rio Grande (in these two cases, Nueva Laredo and Matamoros, respectively). American shoppers flock across the border in search of bargains, and Mexicans cross—illegally as well as legally—in search of jobs and economic opportunity. The North American Free Trade Agreement of the mid-1990s streamlined customs procedures and spurred greater truck traffic across the border throughout the Rio Grande Valley as well. The romantic streets of Laredo, the museums of Harlingen, the lighthouses and wild parrot roosts of Brownsville, the orchards of McAllen, the resort hotels of South Padre Island, the astonishingly vast holdings of the King Ranch (birthplace of American ranching and a spread bigger than Rhode Island), and shops on the Mexican side of the river are magnets for recreational, ecological, and historical tourism alike. This is "winter Texan" country, which is invaded each winter by northerners and Canadians and their automobiles, mobile homes, and recreational vehicles—and deserted just as quickly come summer.

The upper reaches of the Texas Gulf Coast—from Corpus Christi to the largely undeveloped seashore of (north) Padre Island to Galveston—have their own allure. "Corpus" is a city of great bridges, unbelievable sunrises, grand parks and museums, and Texas's state aquarium. Padre Island National Seashore, on the skinny barrier island, is a place of relaxation and imagination with its tales of lost Spanish galleons and vast treasures buried in the sand. Galveston Island is Texas's New Orleans—sultry, historic, and slightly naughty—with a boardwalk and beach. It even holds a Mardi Gras. If New Orleans is "The Big Easy," Galveston—at least for one of its Mardi Gras during

Roy Orbison (center), a shy student with weak eyes and an incredible tenor voice, is caught in a moment of relaxation with his high-school band, the "Wink Westerners," in tiny Wink, Texas.

the 1990s)—was "The Big Speakeasy." Galveston is also Houston's playland. That giant metropolis fifty miles to the northeast has recovered astoundingly from the devastating recession that rocked the oil economy in the late 1980s. Houston has many attractions—most far newer than the San Jacinto obelisk monument that marks the site where Texas won its independence, or the Astrodome, the world's first domed stadium and still a fascinating marvel of engineering. Among them are: the Transco Water Wall, in which water cascades down two arches of a sixty-four-foot, U-shaped fountain; six miles of downtown tunnels for *walkers;* East Houston's *yerberia* herb shops; Holocaust, fire, and even funeral-service museums; the Orange Show, an indescribable tribute to the citrus; and the Beer Can House, adorned with fifty-thousand tinkling beer cans. Like Amarillo, Houston calls itself the "real Texas." Perhaps they'll settle the argument at high noon in Abilene!

Texas's old military garrison of San Antonio—always a tourist favorite—rocketed from pleasant obscurity to international prominence with completion of the *Paseo del Rio*—the River Walk. Below city streets, river cruisers travel the horseshoe bend in the San Antonio River, bordered not only by restaurants, nightclubs, and retail shops but also by towering cypresses, oaks, willows, and gardens full of ornamental plants. Its network of stone paths and stairways to street levels were not new: W.P.A. workers built them in the 1930s. But city planners turned them into an attraction that has been envied—and copied—by communities around the world. Suddenly visitors were moved to discover more than the Alamo and San Antonio's trail of Spanish missions. Art galleries and gardens, the city zoo and old shopping plaza, a new sports arena and new convention center, and museums like the Institute of Texas Cultures have burst to life, capturing the imagination of travelers.

Austin, the state capital—once called Waterloo—has been beautified and modernized. The

During the Great Depression, Arlington, Texas, became a gambler's paradise. W. T. Waggoner, considered the wealthiest man west of the Mississippi, converted part of his ranch into Arlington Downs Race Track.

1886 Driskell Hotel—perhaps Texas's most historic hostelry—for instance, underwent a whole-sale restoration in the late 1990s while retaining the charms of its "guest chambers," grand ballroom, lobby, and "dining hall." The city suggests so many walking tours of its other historic properties that several pamphlets must be printed to cover them all. Yet at the same time, Austin became such a "hot" entertainment center that the city adopted a startling slogan: "Live Music Capital of the World." And Austin is also the logical jumping off point for tours of the nearby Hill Country, including visits to German-influenced Fredericksburg, the LBJ birthplace and ranch, and the somewhat raunchy hangout of "Waylon, Willie, and the Boys" in tiny Luckenbach.

One other small Texas city should not be overlooked—Beaumont. It avoids braggadocio and tends to mind its own business on the banks of the lower Neches River in the East Texas Gulf Coast. Originally settled by both Spanish and French fur trappers in the early 1800s, it is agreeably nestled less than an hour from the Gulf, to the south, and the Big Thicket National Preserve, to the north. This is Texas Cajun country, where Boudreaux is as common a name as Smith or Jones, and the seafood is as spicy as any in Lafayette or Breaux Bridge. Easy does it in Beaumont. As its Convention & Visitors Bureau asks: "Where else can you canoe through the Big Thicket in the afternoon, dine on barbecue crabs while overlooking the gulf, and still en-joy an evening at the racetrack or casino?" Where else, indeed?

Thanks to San Antonio's meteoric growth, Texas now has three of the ten largest cities in America. That's the big news, the kind Texans relish. Of slightly less import, it also has more than two hundred thousand alligators, the world's largest concentration of bats (in Bracken Cave, San Antonio), the tallest Ferris wheel in the Western Hemisphere (at the State Fairgrounds in Dal-las), thirty-seven hundred separate rivers and streams, a state animal (the armadillo), and a state dish (chili). Big, brash, and beautiful, the Lone Star State can be, in the Texas vernacular, a hoot!

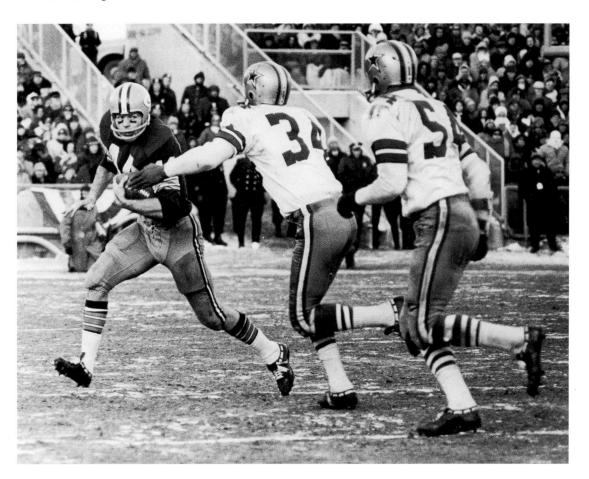

Two of the greatest Dallas Cowboy football players, defensive back Cornell Green (34) and linebacker Chuck Howley (54), pursue the Packers' Donnie Anderson during the 'Boys' infamous 1967 "Ice Bowl" loss to Green Bay.

OVERLEAF: Settlers in the Mexican state of Texas turned the old, limestone Alamo mission into a fortress where they made a heroic but fatal stand for independence in 1836.

"Old (and stuffed) Tex" (above) is the world's largest mounted longhorn, with a horn span of eight feet nine inches. He stands at San Antonio's Buckhorn Museum and Saloon, founded in 1881 by inveterate hunter Albert Friedrich. He built his collection by offering patrons free drinks in exchange for pairs of horns, rattlesnake skins, and stuffed animals of all shapes, sizes, and ferocity. Many of the animals originally featured are now extinct or endangered. Mission San José y San Miguel de Aguayo in San Antonio (right) is regarded as the "Queen of Texas Missions." It was the most prosperous and best fortified of the structures along Mission Trail. Always cooler than the streetscape above, San Antonio's River Walk (overleaf) is especially inviting at breakfast time.

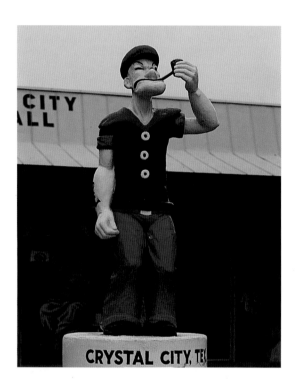

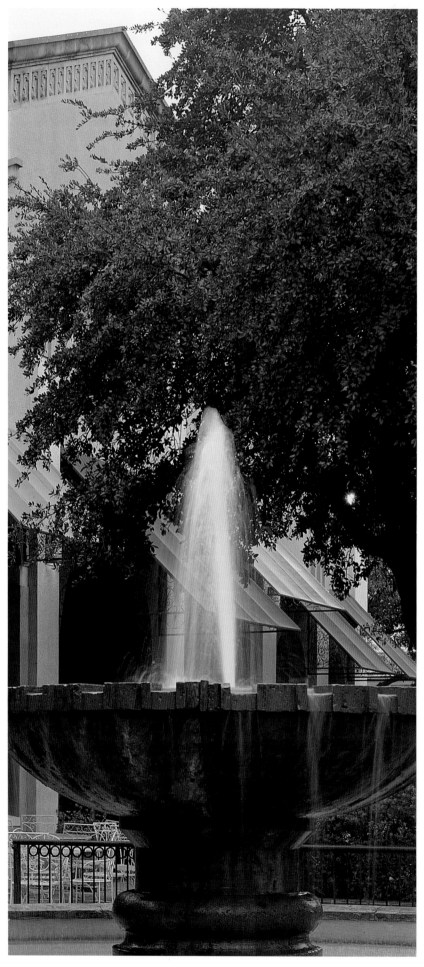

Popeye the Sailor Man (above)—"strong to the finish 'cause I eat my spinach"—dates to 1937, and is an apt symbol of the little South Texas town of Crystal City, near which giant spinach farms thrive. Old City Hall (right) in romantic Laredo in Mercado Plaza is now the Laredo Center for the Arts, home to art exhibitions and outdoor concerts. A statue of Saint Augustine (opposite) stands in a plaza once bordered by high walls to protect the city from Indian raids. Augustine was the patron saint of José de Escandon, who received a grant from Spain to settle the northernmost provinces of New Spain, including Texas.

Quinta Mazatlan (left) in McAllen was built in 1935 by Jason Chilton Matthews, an eccentric soldier of fortune who once fought in the Middle East with Lawrence of Arabia. He and his wife, Marcia, published and edited the ultraconservative American Mercury magazine. The house is the largest remaining adobe hacienda in Texas. Artwork, decorative tile, and stained-glass windows adorn the thirteen-thousand-square-foot mansion. Outside, bougain-villaea, tall palms, lush tropicals, and a boundless cactus garden (above) verify McAllen's nick-name as the "Texas Tropics." Nearby are bountiful orange and grapefruit groves, and sugar-cane fields.

Enjoying an old Mexican birthday and holiday tradition, children at First Baptist School encourage a classmate as she flails at a piñata filled with candies (above) in Brownsville—

the southernmost city in the continental United States. So common are exotic birds—including red-crowned parrots—flying freely in this "city on the border by the sea" that the

Brownsville Convention & Visitors Bureau publishes a birder's guide. Nearby in the little town of Pharr, Smitty's is a world-famous jukebox museum (opposite) and a jukebox repair and

sales shop. Founder Leo "Smitty" Schmitt Sr. makes it clear that his treasured display models— with their "bubbler" neon outlines and mechanisms that still play tunes for

a nickel—are not for sale. The Art Deco masterpieces belt out competing sounds— from Bob Wills's western hit "Stay a Little Longer" to the rock classic "Rock Around the Clock."

The Port Isabel Light-
house (above) near
Brownsville overlooks
Laguna Madre, the
narrow strait between
the Texas Mainland
and South Padre
Island. Built in 1835,
it operated until 1905.
Padre Island is two
distinct land masses,
separated by the
manmade Port
Mansfield Channel
and unconnected by
bridges. South Padre
Island is heavily
developed with a
lively restaurant
and nightlife scene.
Remote Padre
Island—one of
the nation's last
unspoiled stretches
of seashore—makes
up 110 miles of the
longer northern finger
of the island, accessed
by causeway from
Corpus Christi.
Intriguing seashells
and glass bottles from
across the sea are rou-
tinely discovered on
the island's Malaquite
Beach (right).

Corpus Christi, midway up the Texas Gulf coastline, is a city of bridges, including the spectacular Harbor Bridge (opposite) connecting downtown to Corpus Christi Beach and the Texas State Aquarium. "Corpus," as Texans shorten the name, is also home to the Art Museum of South Texas; a museum of science and history that exhibits replicas of Christopher Columbus's Nina, Pinta, and Santa Maria; and delightful Heritage Park, a downtown block to which fascinating historic homes have been moved from throughout the area. North of town in tiny Rockport is the Fulton Mansion (left), an elaborate French Second Empire–style home completed in 1877. Cattle baron George W. Fulton's Victorian showplace featured the latest conveniences, including gas lights fueled by his own natural-gas plant at the rear of the house.

The King Ranch sprawls across 825,000 acres of South Texas, an area larger than Rhode Island. On a map, it's a huge, empty white space. Driving through it at night, it's a vast black expanse, the ranch's sixty thousand cattle unseen until morning. Each year, the ranch throws a cowboy breakfast (above), open to the Kingsville community and visitors. Mixing pancake batter are, left to right, Tio Kleberg, Tom B. Saunders, Jay Evans, and Nicho Morales. Volunteers David Pratt and Madelyn Ahrens patrol the event on horseback (opposite), pausing in front of an old building from the days when the King spread was called the Santa Gertrudis Ranch. Civilization is very much in evidence in revitalized Houston (overleaf), which has snapped back from a devastating oil recession with a vengeance. The "real Texas," as Houston calls itself, has become a model of ethnic diversity.

SHUTTLE

APOLLO

LUNAR EVA SUIT

This exact suit was worn by Charles "Pete" Conrad
as he walked on the moon during the Apollo 12 mission.

CONRAD

NASA

A veteran of two Gemini flights, Charles "Pete" Conrad was Mission Commander for the November, 1969 Apollo 12 expedition. A native Philadelphian and a Princeton graduate, Conrad followed Armstrong and Aldrin and became the third man to walk on the Moon. Traveling aboard the Lunar Module Intrepid—Conrad and Lunar Module Pilot Alan Bean landed on the Moon at the Ocean of Storms, just a few feet away from the unmanned Surveyor 3 spacecraft that had nestled down onto the lunar surface two and a half years earlier. The Apollo 12 Moon landing was an extremely challenging maneuver and was considered one of the most precise landings in the history of navigation.

Once Conrad planted his feet on the Moon, he loped around in high spirits as he became accustomed to the lunar gravity. A flurry of Moon dust made their work difficult as Conrad and Bean set up the Apollo Lunar Surface Experiment Package (ALSEP) during their first extravehicular activity which lasted approximately four hours.

Once the ALSEP started operating, Conrad and Bean began the exciting work of Moon rock collecting. Conrad described one sample as "a pure piece of glass," and after a second Moonwalk, the two astronauts collected a total of about 75 pounds of material. Apollo 12 did not have the worldwide attention of Apollo 11's first Moon landing, but it proved that venturing to this new world would happen again, and that even more exciting explorations of space were on the horizon.

SULLIVAN

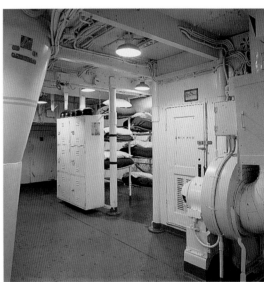

Space Center Houston (left) is a showcase for America's space program. This interactive visitor center for NASA's Johnson Space Center takes guests into the past, present, and future of the nation's astronaut program, with space shuttle mock-ups, IMAX films, and a glimpse of the astronauts in weightlessness training. One of the rites of Texas youth is a pilgrimage to the USS battleship Texas (above), moored in the marshes off Houston's San Jacinto Park. The ship, once the world's most powerful dreadnought, survived a U-boat attack in World War I and supported landings at Normandy and Okinawa in World War II. The Houston Astrodome (overleaf) was the world's first domed stadium when it opened in 1965. It's home to the Houston Astros baseball team, rodeos, and trade shows.

Galveston Island is Texas's playland and languid antebellum retreat. Homes like the 1896 Maud Moller House (above), with its unusual curving stairway, fill the city's East End Historical District. Galveston's Downtown Revitalization Coalition has returned the historic Strand area into a bustling neighborhood reminiscent of the days when Galveston was known as "The Wall Street of the South"—before the "Great Storm" of 1900 wiped out much of the city. The ten-story Rainforest Pyramid (right) is a place where butterflies, birds, and tropical fish share the environment with exotic plants. It is a highlight of Galveston's Moody Gardens, which has grown from a simple horse barn and riding arena into a sprawling educational and recreational complex of gardens, greenhouses, and therapy centers for persons with physical and emotional disabilities.

The Gladys City Boomtown Museum (above) in Beaumont recalls the days when Spindletop Hill covered a vast pool of oil. The Gladys City Company was the first oil company to drill there in 1893—with no success. But on January 10, 1901, Anthony Lucas, an Austrian-born mining engineer, struck oil. The Lucas Gusher sprayed "black gold" more than one hundred feet above a derrick for nine days until the well was capped. (See a historic view of the gusher on page 14.) Gladys City Boomtown was a city bicentennial project; the complex was given to the state and Lamar University for continued care and development as an educational resource about the great early-1900s oil boom. Near the little town of Brenham, Franciscan Poor Clare nuns at the Saint Clare Monastery support their cloistered contemplation by raising miniature horses (opposite) and making altar beads.

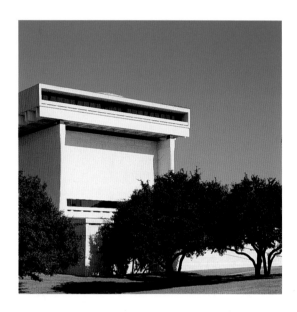

The Lyndon B. Johnson Library (above) in Austin is the nation's largest and most-visited presidential library. It includes a full-scale replica of the White House Oval Office. Regrettably, the twenty-seven-story University Tower (right), the University of Texas's signature building on its 357-acre Austin campus, has become irrevocably associated with a tragedy: the day in 1966 when deranged honor student Charles Whitman shot forty-four people, killing fourteen, from the Tower's parapet before being shot dead by an off-duty policeman. The dome of the Texas State Capitol (opposite)—the largest state capitol building in the nation—rises seven feet taller than the U.S. Capitol in Washington. The ceiling of the capitol rotunda (overleaf) highlights the Lone Star—the symbol of the Texas Republic.

The Greek Revival Texas Governor's Mansion (above) was constructed of local handmade bricks. Pine logs hauled from Bastrop, Texas, were used to form its six massive pillars. When the mansion opened in 1856, Governor Elisha Pease threw such a "gay and brilliant affair" for three hundred guests that it took him three days to clean up. Pease kept the American Empire sofa, now in the library (opposite), at his private home. Stephen F. Austin's desk occupies another corner. Furnishings have departed, too. Among the possessions that Sam Houston carted home were seventy-five pounds of feathers and eight spittoons. Until Governor John Connally's wife, Idanell, pushed to get an iron fence, brick wall, and security outposts around the mansion, anyone could— and often did— ring the doorbell and roust the governor's family for a chat and an impromptu peek at Houston's old bedroom.

Texans love their Hill Country in the central part of the state, west of Austin. President and Mrs. Lyndon B. Johnson, for instance, returned to their modest home (left) on their working ranch along the Pedernales River at every opportunity. Although Fredericksburg was founded in 1846 by German settlers and retains its German architecture and cuisine in several locations, other European pioneers put their stamp on the community as well. In 1864, Belgian native Felix Van Der Stricken, owner of the town's water-powered gristmill, built his home (above)—now the Market Square Bed & Breakfast Inn—out of native limestone. The bare spot in the distance (overleaf) is the Enchanted Rock State Natural Area, one of Texans' favorite hiking and picnicking areas.

Texas Agricultural and Mechanical, or Texas A&M, University in College Station (above), founded in 1876, is the oldest state university in Texas. It is famed for its military Cadet Corps and ROTC programs, whose graduates served by the thousands in both World Wars, the Korean War, and in Vietnam and Iraq. A&M students good-naturedly bear the bumpkin image as "Aggies," but the nickname belies the school's leadership in agriculture, engineer-ing, and nuclear tech-nology. The George Bush Presidential Library and Museum (left) opened on the Texas A&M Univer-sity campus in College Station in 1997. Its exhibits range from a 1925 home movie of Bush's first steps in Kennebunkport, Maine, to mementos of his leadership during Operation Desert Storm. Another section is dedicated to First Lady Barbara Bush's efforts on behalf of literacy, AIDS prevention, and volunteerism.

SAM HOUSTON
1793 - 1863

The monumental statue of Texas hero Sam Houston (above) at the Huntsville visitors' center can be seen from as far as six miles away. David Adickes created the sixty-seven-foot statue out of thirty tons of steel and concrete. "Old Sparky" (opposite), Texas's infamous electric chair in which 361 inmates were executed from 1924 to 1964, was moved to the Texas Prison Museum in Huntsville in 1989. One doomed convict, J.W. Moore Jr., ordered for his last meal "a small steak, tender, no bone, no fat" plus French fries, butter beans, steak sauce, sliced onion, five large bananas, chocolate ice cream, and one piece of fluffy coconut pie. "Dammit," he wrote, "I want it served hot, and keep it from being mixed up together."

THE TEXAS ELECTRIC CHAIR

"Old Sparky," was used
to execute 361 inmates
from 1924 to 1964. It
was then crated and
stored near the execution
room in the Walls Unit
until it was moved to the
Texas Prison Museum in
April 1989. Executions
were resumed in Texas in
1982 with the lethal
injection method.

The Dr Pepper Museum (opposite) in the beverage's old bottling plant in Waco is a delightful repository of information and artifacts from the entire soft-drink industry. Between pours of Dr Pepper, executive director Joe Cavanaugh tells the story of pharmacist Charles Curtis Alderton's creation of the soda pop in 1885. In Lufkin is the Texas Forestry Museum (top left), which displays early logging machinery, firefighting equipment and a fire tower, and a sawmill town exhibit. Caddo Lake (bottom left) has all the earmarks of a Louisiana swamp, including cypress trees draped in Spanish moss.

Tyler, the "Rose Capital of the Nation," maintains the country's largest municipal rose garden and museum (above). The combination of year-round rainfall, sandy soil, and a long growing season makes Tyler ideal for rose propagation. Roses were first produced commercially here in the 1870s. Four signers of the Texas Declaration of Independence are buried in Oak Grove Cemetery (opposite) in Nacogdoches, arguably Texas's most historic town. It sat on the Texas side of a "no man's land" separating Spain's New World colonies from French Louisiana, so it was a hotbed of smuggling and revolutionary intrigue. Freedom fighters heading for the Alamo were fêted in Nacogdoches on the way to their fateful encounter with Santa Anna's Mexican troops. The East Texas Oil Museum at Kilgore College maintains a street scene (overleaf) that vividly illustrates some of the vicissitudes of life in an oil boomtown.

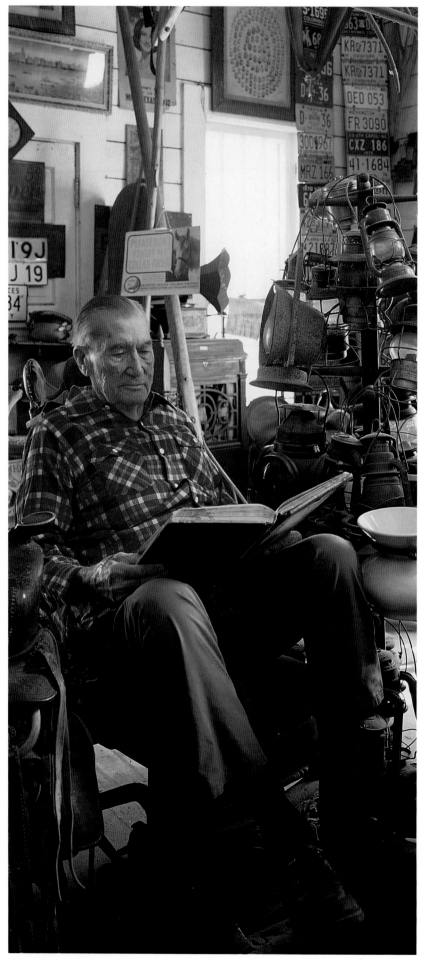

White Oak Manor (above) is one of more than sixty bed-and-breakfast inns in tiny Jefferson, a favorite East Texas escape destination for folks in the Dallas–Fort Worth Metroplex. The white oak out front is older than the house, which dates to 1887. Octogenarian owner Tom Vaughan takes a gander at an 1885 ledger from Jonesville's T. C. Lindsey General Store (right), which was founded in 1847 by his great uncle on the stagecoach road between Marshall and Caddo Lake. Many antique collections are on display at the store, which sells hard-to-find hardware doodads. The Gregg County Historical Museum (opposite), in the 1910 Everett bank building in Longview, traces the county's colorful history and maintains a complete guide to its many historical markers.

Texarkana's post office (above) was constructed on Stateline Avenue—straddling the Texas-Arkansas line. Even the flag of the United States is bisected by the state boundary. Federal courts for both states convene on their respective sides of the building. Olivia Smith Moore, wife of Texarkana attorney Henry Moore, acquired an impressive shoe collection (opposite), still displayed in the bedroom at Texarkana's famous Draughon-Moore "Ace of Clubs" house. She amassed more than five hundred pairs of shoes, plus other fine clothing brought to her door by sales representatives from the Neiman-Marcus store in Dallas. Lumberman James Draughon built the home in 1885 in the shape of the ace of clubs, his lucky card from his days as a Confederate Army captain. According to legend, money to build the house came from a poker game won with the draw of that card.

Country music superstar Clint Black (above) strummed his guitar in front of the courthouse in McKinney, north of Dallas, during the filming of a music video. One of Texas's most impressive courthouses can be found in nearby Denton (opposite), the "North Star of Texas." Others call it "Little D," in contrast to the metropolis down the road. The walls of the 1896 courthouse are native limestone, the columns of Burnett County marble. Architect W.C. Dodson's design is a free combination of Victorian styles. Inside is the Courthouse-on-Square museum, which displays Victorian rooms as well as period guns, pottery, dolls, tools, and blue glass. The museum is also a center for North Texas genealogical research. Dallas's skyline (overleaf) shimmers with the energy that turned "Big D" from a sleepy trading post into one of the nation's most powerful, and architecturally imaginative, business centers seemingly overnight.

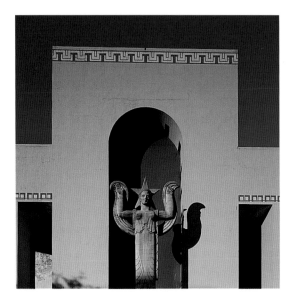

Lone Star, *one of six massive statues (above) representing the six nations that have administered Texas, stands before an Art Deco building along the esplanade in Dallas's Fair Park, built for the huge 1936 exposition. It commemorated the Texas centennial, which seven million people attended. Now rented space, the 84,000-square-foot building houses the annual display of antique automobiles during the gigantic state fair—the world's largest and possibly its longest—over three weeks each September and October. The 277-acre Fair Park includes the largest collection of Art Deco architecture in the United States. Many of Dallas's business elite have built magnificent homes in the North Park section (right), site of beautiful urban parks and one of the nation's first planned suburban shopping centers.*

After years of shame over the twist of fate that cast it as the site of the 1963 assassination of President John F. Kennedy, Dallas has squarely confronted the memory with a powerful exhibit in the Texas School Book Depository Building (above). Visitors to the Sixth Floor Museum get a full recounting of the events of that November day and an eerily familiar view of Dealey Plaza (left) from the window next to the one from which— according to the official Warren Commission account— lone assassin Lee Harvey Oswald drew a bead on the president and Governor John Connally. The rest of the building houses Dallas County's administration.

A small log cabin (above) was moved from the countryside seven miles outside of town to downtown Dallas, then to its present spot on Historic Square in 1971. Named for settler George Mifflin Dallas of Pennsylvania, Dallas was little more than a post office in the Texas Republic of 1845. Most colonists called the area along the Trinity River "Three Forks," and surely no one dreamed that one day, Dallas would grow into one of the nation's most dynamic supercities. Pioneer Plaza (right) in downtown Dallas is the world's largest bronze monument. Its seventy longhorn steers (forty of which were first unveiled during World Cup soccer festivities in 1994) and three cowboys commemorate the city's western heritage. Robert Summers of Glen Rose, Texas, created the sculptures.

In Williams Square—the center of the Metroplex's "alternate downtown" in Irving—Robert Glen created the powerful Mustangs of Las Colinas *sculptures (left) that have become a favorite attraction. The Texas Rangers' intimate, state-of-the-art Ballpark (above) combines with two Six Flags Over Texas theme parks to bring thousands of visitors to Arlington. Billy Bob's Texas in Fort Worth (overleaf)—"The World's Largest Honky Tonk"—opened in 1981 in a building that was once an open-air barn housing prize cattle for the Fort Worth Stock Show. In the 1950s, it became a department store so large that stockboys wore roller skates. For one Hank Williams Jr. concert in the 6,028-seat club, Billy Bob's sold more than sixteen thousand bottles of beer.*

MAIN
SHOW ROOM

FORT WO[RTH]

1867   CHISHOLM   TRAIL

The Chisholm Trail, which established Fort Worth as "Cowtown" as hundreds of thousands of longhorns were herded from South Texas to the Abilene, Kansas, railhead after the Civil War, is remembered in Richard Haas's spectacular mural (left) in Fort Worth's Sundance Square. The square was once the heart of the city's raucous "Hell's Half Acre" of saloons and gambling halls where cowpokes stopped for one last fling before heading north across Indian Territory toward Kansas. Mike Smith (above) owns the Paris Coffee Shop, a Fort Worth culinary legend since its opening in 1930. Home cooking—from chicken-fried steaks and biscuits with sausage gravy, to a dozen kinds of pies—is a tradition at the humble diner that draws patrons from all over North Texas.

A statue outside Wichita Falls's Municipal Auditorium (opposite) was dedicated to "the War with Spain, Philippines, and China Nanking Expedition of 1898–1902." In other words, to the U.S. veterans of the Spanish-American War. The Wichita Falls Symphony and Ballet as well as country-and-western artists perform at the auditorium, which hosts more than eighty events annually. To replace the city's namesake falls, which washed away more than one hundred years ago, a nearby fifty-four-foot manmade falls was constructed in 1986.

At a state historical park near Abilene and Albany on the site of the 1867–81 Fort Griffin, the Texas Department of Parks & Wildlife raises longhorn steers like this baleful beast (above). Several remnants of the fort, from which soldiers headed out on dangerous campaigns against hostile Indians roaming the High Plains to the north and west, still stand.

Three buildings and a dozen chimneys remain from Fort Phantom Hill (above) near Abilene. It billeted five companies of infantry for only three years in the 1850s before being abandoned. The fort came to be called Fort Phantom Hill for a hill that rises sharply from the plains but seems to retreat like a phantom when approached. A surrounding town disappeared when the county seat and railroad line were located elsewhere. In 1892, a San Antonio newspaper wrote that Phantom Hill had "one hotel, one saloon, one general store, one blacksmith shop and 10,000 prairie dogs." Near Albany in Shackelford County, a windmill (opposite) stands at the site of an old stage line and pony express stop. The "Greasy Spoon" (overleaf) is a fanciful remnant of "America's Main Street" in the Route 66 Museum in tiny McLean, east of Amarillo, in the Texas Panhandle.

In the same building in McLean that houses the Route 66 Museum (see page 92) is the Devil's Rope Museum (opposite), an exhaustive collection of barbed wire, tools used to stretch it, and sculptures made from it. Indians called barbed wire the "devil's rope" because it restrained their movement; settlers called it "bob wire"; cattlemen cursed it; and range wars were fought where it was strung. Cowboy Mike Dean (above) gets a grip on one of the most bizarre monuments in Texas at the Cadillac Ranch near Amarillo. There, eccentric helium tycoon Stanley Marsh III—with help from a San Francisco design firm called the Ant Farm—buried ten 1949–63 model Cadillacs nose down. The rusting frames soon became a favorite target of graffiti artists. What does it all mean? Guessing is half the fun.

"Trophy buckles" (above)—ornate belt buckles worn by cowboys and often presented as rodeo prizes—are a popular item at Cavender's Boot City western-wear store in Amarillo. Boots (left), of course, which range in price from $39 to more than $1,400, are the biggest sellers. Just about everyone in town wears them everywhere. South of Amarillo is the eight-hundred-foot-deep Palo Duro Canyon (overleaf)—the nation's second-largest canyon—whose copper-colored cliffs are especially spectacular at sunset.

Hodie Porterfield takes "the challenge" at the Big Texan Steak Ranch (opposite) in Amarillo, as Linda Roybal looks on. The challenge, familiar to many visitors whose eyes are far bigger than their stomachs: if you can finish a seventy-two-ounce steak—the size of a small roast!—and all the trimmings, the meal is free. Hundreds of people have done it; amazingly, many have been women or slightly built men. John Russell Thomasson painted the mural (top left) outside Roadhouse Ruby's, a popular Lubbock country-and-western night club. The visage of the late Roy Orbison (bottom left) appears on a wall outside the tiny museum devoted to the early rock-'n'-roll superstar in his hometown of Wink, just below the Texas Panhandle. Tina Rasco created this mural.

Large petrochemical complexes abound in the old Texas oil patch. This Ameripol Synpol Corporation plant (above) in Odessa makes synthetic rubber from the byproducts left by a nearby plant's production of Styrofoam. Almost as common as sagebrush on the West Texas plains are pumpjacks like the one (opposite) near Penwell. Pumpjacks go to work long after the "gusher" stage of a well, sucking the dregs of oil from the rocks beneath the desert. So that all who have mineral rights may have fair access to the oil below, the government mandates that the 'jacks' hours of operation be staggered. Near the state line toward the southeastern corner of New Mexico is Monahans Sandhills State Park (overleaf), consisting of 3,840 acres of dunes up to seventy feet high. Many are stabilized by vegetation, but bare, active dunes grow and change shape in response to prevailing winds.

Branding is a twice-a-year ritual (left) on big cattle spreads like the Ratliff Cross MX Ranch near Odessa. Calves are branded and inoculated against a variety of diseases, and males are castrated. "Jalepeño Sam" Lewis (above) raises and races armadillos like "Tex." The little burrowing mammals, which one wag called "anteaters on the half shell," often become road kill, or "Texas speed bumps," not because they dawdle but because, when cornered by an oncoming car, they tend to hop upward, striking the undercarriage. Midland's wildly popular young Ballet Folk Dancers (overleaf), here performing at Ninfa's Restaurant, learn dance—and self-confidence—at the Hispanic Cultural Center of Midland.

Fort Concho (opposite) in San Angelo is nearly as active today as it was at the end of the nineteenth century. Costumed interpreters demonstrate daily frontier life, and the

garrison comes to life during special events. Among those once stationed there were companies of black soldiers known respectfully by their Indian enemies as "buffalo soldiers."

Deer hunting is so good in West Texas that hunters fly in from around the world to test their skills. At the popular Adobe Lodge Hunting Camp (above) near San Angelo, Blake

Duncan takes aim while his father—the ranch's owner, Skipper Duncan—demonstrates one of a guide's favorite tricks: rattling deer antlers. This simulates the sound of

two bucks contesting territory, which can arouse the ire of the buck who had staked out that turf. When he hurries over to investigate, he barges into the hunter's gunsight.

Del Rio's Val Verde Winery (above), Texas's oldest bonded winery, has been making wine continuously since 1883, when Italian immigrant Frank Qualia began the family business.

A third generation of Qualias now produces wines, notably a Don Luis tawny port that has won medals from Houston to New York. Across the Pecos River in tiny Langtry, the state operates a visitor center on the site of "Judge" Roy Bean's old courthouse (opposite)—which was more often a saloon. (For a look at hizzoner, see the historic photograph on page 9.) Not far away is Seminole Canyon State Historical Park, where some of North America's oldest cave pictographs (overleaf), believed to have been painted four thousand years ago, have been carefully preserved. One reason why vandals have not desecrated the site: it's concealed from easy view and reachable only after a strenuous—and well supervised—hike.

Though "the skies are not cloudy all day" in dry West Texas, roiling clouds mixed with sun are a common sight, as in this scene (opposite) near Saragosa. The Davis Mountains loom in the distance. Rocky crests are closer to the highway in Big Bend National Park (above). The park, which was established along the serpentine curve of the Rio Grande River to protect the fragile Chihuahuan Desert wilderness, covers eleven hundred square miles. The park's vast basins and weathered mountains are full of self-guided trails, but supplies and especially accommodations are relatively scarce. The rugged Chisos Mountains that rise abruptly out of the plains were formed by ancient volcanos. Elsewhere, molten lava squeezed through sedimentary rock to the earth's surface. There is ample evidence throughout the park, too, of violent flash floods. In all, the effect can be awe-inspiring.

Metal craftsman Clayton Parker creates silhouettes and western scenes like the bull (top right) and the windmill climber (opposite) by hand in his Art of Iron shop in Fort Stockton. His handiwork appears in the distinctive displays that Texas ranchers mount above their entrance gates. Road-runner "Paisano Pete" (bottom right)—eleven feet tall and twenty-two feet long—is the symbol of Fort Stockton. There was a fort in Fort Stockton from 1867 to 1886, serving the usual frontier-outpost role. An earlier camp on the site was briefly occupied by Con-federate forces during the Civil War. Centrally located between the New Mexico border and Big Bend National Park, Fort Stockton is a good base for touring the park, the Carlsbad Caverns, the Davis Mountains, and the Monahans sand dunes.

The McDonald Observatory (left and above) near Fort Davis is operated by the University of Texas at Austin. Its twin telescopes sit on Mount Locke atop the highest point on any Texas highway, 6,791 feet above sea level and 2,500 feet above the valley below. Solar viewing sessions are conducted daily at 11 A.M. and 3:30 P.M. using a telescope equipped with a filtered lens and a video camera to observe the sun's features. On Wednesday evenings closest to a full moon, the observatory gives visitors a rare opportunity to view the stars through the world's largest publicly accessible telescope. And on Tuesday, Friday, and Saturday at sunset at the public observatory behind the visitor center, the observatory hosts "star parties."

*Half the original
structures, and many
ruins, remain from
historic Fort Davis
(above) where, from
1854 to 1891, troops
based at the post
battled Apache and
Comanche Indians.*

*They also escorted
freight wagons, stage-
coaches, and pioneers
heading to the new
American territories
in New Mexico and
Arizona on the bleak
San Antonio-to-
El Paso Trail. The*

*fort was named for
Secretary of War—
later Confederate
president—Jefferson
Davis. The Ysleta
Mission (opposite) in
suburban El Paso was
built in 1681 by Fran-
ciscan priests and*

*Tigua Indians. The
building has been
reconstructed but
stands on the original
foundation and is
therefore considered to
be the oldest mission
in Texas. It is again
attended by Tiguas—*

*descendants of the
tribe that built it more
than three centuries
ago. Near El Paso the
desert (overleaf) is
enchanting much of
the year but broiling
and forbidding in
summertime.*

Index

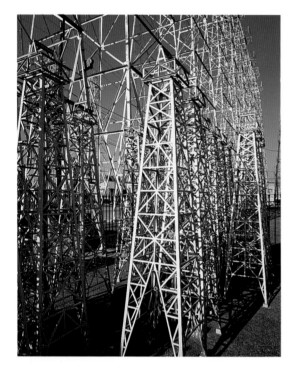

Full-size and scaled-down models of oil derricks mark a sliver of the "World's Richest Acre" that has been preserved in downtown Kilgore. The block was the most densely drilled tract in the world. One acre yielded more than 2.5 million barrels of crude oil—earning $5.5 million— beginning in 1937.